YARDBIRD SUITE

Side One: 1920-1940

YARDBIRD SUITE
Side One: 1920-1940

A Biopoem
Fictionalized Accounts of Events
Real and Imagined
in the Life of
CHARLES "YARDBIRD" PARKER
Jazz Musician
19 August 1920-
12 March 1955

by
Bill Harris

Michigan State University Press
East Lansing

Michigan State University Press
East Lansing, Michigan 48823-5202

03 02 01 00 99 98 97   1 2 3 4 5 6 7 8 9

Library of Congress Cataloging-in-Publication Data

Harris, Bill, 1941-
        Yardbird suite : side one—1920-1940 / by Bill harris
            p.   cm. — (Lotus Poetry Series)
    "A biopoem, fictionalized accounts of events real and imagined from the life of Charles 'Yardbird' Parker, jazz musician, 19 August 1920-12 March 1955."
        ISBN 0-87013-435-3
        1. Parker, Charlie, 1920-1955—Poetry. 2. Jazz musicians—United States—Poetry. 3. Afro-American musicians—Poetry. I. Title. II. Series.

PS3558.A6415Y37   1997
811'.54—dc21
                                                            907-45585
                                                            CIP
                                                            r97

Lotus Poetry Series Editor: Naomi Long Madgett

Acknowledgment is made to the following publications, in which the listed poems, in their original versions, first appeared: *Style* for "'Round Midnight: Bed Time"; *Eyeball* for "Hallelujah"; and *The World* for "Hot House: 1515 Oliver Street K.C., Mo.," "Home Cookin': Charles and Rebecca. Their Bedroom. Evening," "Dark Shadows: Nighthawks," and "Back Home Blues."

"Music,"
Bird learned,
"is your own experience,
your thoughts,

your wisdom.
If you don't live it, it
won't
come out of your horn."

CONTENTS

NOTES: All poem titles are titles of tunes recorded by Parker during
       his career.
       Marginal numbers refer to the author's end notes.
       An asterisk (*) at the end or beginning of a page indicates a
       stanza break.

Ornithology:
Genealogy
circa 1919

1. "Oh, my," Addie,
budding country gal
from across Kaycee's Kaw   1
thought, listening to him.

And he, Charles Parker,
roving eyed, fickle-
footed stroller through
an orchard of such
women, talking his
ivory tinkling, rib
tickling, toe tapping
browneyed big-time talk.

"Oh, my," shiny eyed,
blossoming Addie,
Temptation Tree fruit,
thought. "Oh, oh my my."   2

2. She was Baptist.
She was 17.
She became his bride.

Body and Soul
         (Take 1)

(29 August,
1920) Charles,
Junior: the cutest
and prettiest child
Addie'd ever seen.
Apple of her eye.
Her reason. Sugar
in her coffee. Her
heart. Her big boy.
Her little man. Would
live, she said, for him.

I'll Always Love You Just the Same

1. ADDIE

Framed on the mantle
near the cut glass vase
with the barely detectable
chip at the base,
her champion on a hobble horse
rides herd on the *bal* of glazed
figurines in tails and gowns;
Charles Junior, aged 2,
in Peter Pan smock
and patent leather Buster Browns.

"Hold on tight. Hold tight,
my honey," Addie
warned, made a funny-
face. "Smile." (A charmer
even then, he did.)

Shutter's quick flutter-
flick! "That's mama's good
boy. Now, let the nice
man help you down." Charles
clung to the reins. Cried.
"A moment more," she
implored the man. Knows
she will deny him
nothing, will bestow
his every wish and whim.

(Colored Kaycee boys
get *so* little . . .) Will

3

be his stitch in Time;
his anodyne to
meanness, mock and might;
cod liver oil for
his every sniffle,
sugared castor oil
for colds. Will forgive
pirated cookies,
prize pranks, and fibs; will
let him be a boy.

Will try and try to
temper her dotage,
rule him with sterner
stroke; say no, she thinks,
while her heart sings (as
it always will), yes!
Yes, little man, yes,
my heavens yes, my
honey, oh yes yes
yes and yes. 2. CHAN   3

Night life lady; hip
as a white woman
could hope to be; knew
jazz from jive; was to
be his wife but not
his wife; told the tale:
her Bronze Buckaroo
come a-courting: " . . . a
colored man on a
palomino to
see you," announced one
(*circa* '51)
night; a prank, kicks. A

living photograph.
Loved her hip jester
for the gesture, the
innocence of it
all . . . 3. ADDIE "Hang

on, tight. Smile. Ride
'em my little man,
my candy cowboy, my
only reason. Ride
'em, and hold on tight."

I Found a New Baby
                circa 1924

Fairskinned, even in
her front room's evening
dim, the boy hangs back.

Charles Junior sits on
the settee, eyes his
parents and the boy.

Bathed in her gaze, Charles
Senior's slanty smile
seems to take a week.

"I'm got to go off."

Then, sheepish as he's
shown adds: "I'm giving
up the life — going
back to cooking on
my old Pullman line.

You know his mama
ain't much count — Well, we
talked on it, agreed
he'll get the better
raising 'neath your hand."

The fair boy chews at
his lip, brushes at
his straight hair, clutches
at his bundled things.
*

"She come to mope or
nose around," says Charles
Senior, "just remind
her I done said, 'Naw.'"

His head motion to
the boy's like a shove.

Grins at each of them.
"Send something first chance . . ."
then eases his hat
on, rakish, and leaves
his drunkard's breath and
the fair boy behind.

"Come here, sugar," she
says, "come stand here in
the light and tell me
what's your name." "Ikey."   4

"That's what they call you,
but your real name's John."

"Yes'm." "I know," she

says, searching his face
for Charles Senior and
his wild wop-woman;
can only find the
least of each of them.
*

"Charles Junior, meet your
brother," then hugs the
fair boy to her, just
like he is her own.

I Remember You

circa 1924

Down on her knees be-
side her bed. O, yes,

Jesus loves her; is
her light brown man with
his dark brown eyes caused
her blues. — Not minted

for no sanctified
or everlasting
love, a Saturday
night not no Sunday
morning kind of man.

His sepia snap-
shot haunted her from
her bureau mirror's
frame. Lord, his parents

must have been pretty,
even his uncles
and his cousins, too.

Hair slick and wavy,
mustache, a pencil
line along his lip.

Knew he cockahoop
strutted, just by his
smile. Brought tender to
*

her life, God bless him.
Baptized her Baby,
accepted her far
from yellowness, her
tangle textured hair . . .

No mind. Toted all

that soft off with him
when that whistle blew
and he got on board.
Needn't be stud'in'
about him no more
no how.
I got Charles

Junior, and Ikey,
got my Usher Board,
my Sunday service,
my prayer meetings on
Wednesday nights — No, Lord,

he wasn't minted
for no sanctified
or everlasting
love — and my mind's stayed
on Jesus. Lord's my

shepherd, and God bless
him, I shall not want . . .

Get Happy:
Mondays and Thursdays
the Deacon's Days to Call

circa late 1920s

1. Stops short, his cry
wadded in his throat;
listens, with new fear,
for the sound again
through her locked-tight bed-
room door: catch of breath?

"Mama?" he whispers,
his scraped-kneed excuse
for intrusion out
of mind. Tips closer;

heart a tambourine
in the joy-frantic
grip of an Amen
corner whooper. Hears

the deacon moan, "My
God! I swear I see
the saints!" "*Yes!*" she groans
with him, as at her
pastor's entreaty
or stirring hymnal
verse. "Mama." Loud this

time; enough for them
to hear. "Mama, you
*

all right?" as he bams
her door. Their movements

sudden as rodents
in the walls, mutters
too quick and low to
understand. "Are you

okay," he calls. " — Yes —

Yes, Mother is fine —
She has company.

Now go away and
play."— "What y'all doing?"

"I told you, I am
not to be disturbed."

Twisting at the knob.

"I need you. I fell,
skint my knee," he whines,
remembering, "and
it hurts. Real bad. Now
you let me in. I
want to see." "*Charles*," her

voice a leaf-stripped switch,
"it will be all right.
Now do what Mother
says!" ". . . It hurts real bad . . ."
*

he whispers, begast
at this first ever
forsaken plea. 2.

Soon, the deacon gone,
she tends to his knee.

"It still hurts," he pouts,
after checking to
confirm it was the
one that had. "I know.

Now how can Mother
make it up to you?"

"Next time," he says, "you
mustn't lock the door."

Lonely Boy Blues
circa 1928

1.

Charles, solitary sentry,
watching.
Ikey, half brother,
keeper — against Addie's strict-
est orders — gone. His, "Be right
back"
a big old fib.
Watching
the permissible porch, the
outer boundary front yard, the
forbidden, shortshadowed
street. Waits. Feels (an unlearned word)
exiled. Feels centuries old.

The swarm of mannish ragtags
shred the sunshine. They buzz and
dart, tempted to the nectar
of a track-side vacant lot.
Will roughhouse, raise sand, vie for
Hilltopper Most Majestic.
A forbidden arena
for Addie's boy, butterball big
in his short trousered suits.
Shoot marbles, Addie'd said,
that's nice.

On their return, tattered, skint
and loud, they bump, brag, dare the
dozens; don't bother to jeer

or even nod.
Stung, he sticks
out his tongue, touches the thread-
thin squarepatterned strands, tastes
the latched screen's metallic gray.

And watching for Addie, waits.

2.

"'M'o' tellll. 'Cause my mama
made you watch after me, 'n'
still you lef' me by myse'f —

So, you to blame," Charles pules.

Ikey eyes the mantle of
beheaded figurines and says,
"You done it deliberate,
didn't you, and she's goin'
know it too." Sings: "Goin'
beat you like a tambourine,
light you up like kerosene,
cut on your young butt like a
guillotine, that's what mama's
going to do to you, that
sure is what she's goin' do."
*

3.

"By yourself?" she says. "Aww, now,
how Mama going
spank her little man
after he had to stay here
all by himself?"

My Heart Belongs to Daddy
circa 1929

1
"Take me," Charlie says,
his tone assuming
his bidding will be done.

Ikey's "No"
is precise
as the tap
of a tuning fork.

"You promised . . ." Nearer now
to the pitch Ikey,
attentive as a tuner
to a concert grand,
is listening for. "No."

"Yes you did, . . ." a quaver.
"The last time you went . . ."

'Better,' Ikey, thinks.
The high-tone nearly gone,
but still not meek enough.
Still too
Mama's Boy.

'Mannish!'
their mother had confided
about her second son's
latest stage. 'Next
he'll be shooting pool.'
*

          "I'll
        tell her
     you go see him
    all the time," but
 without heat or a tinge
     of the tone.

     "I don't care." Ikey's face
   a shield of nonchalance. A look
 Charlie has seen on older men (their
   father even, when he wasn't
       'in his sin'); men
    relaxed, among themselves;
    greeting passing women
  or officers of the law. A look
        he loves.

 "He's my daddy," Ikey adds. "See 'im
     when I want to. Any-
       body don't like it,
     just too black-ass bad."

     Mannish! Mannish,
   Charlie thinks, the awe,
 the affection blazing in his eyes,
        hot-bright
   as Kaycee's setting sun.

      Ikey smiles,
       thinking
     he has won . . .
          *

2

"He's my daddy, too,"
Charles says, playing
the trump card
he didn't know was in his hand.
Says it instinctively,
charged (at that
moment) with utter but guile-
less conviction; composed
of intriguing desire
and naked need. A tone
he will hone, wield
on pushers, club owners, sidemen,
women, the authorities, and fans.

Ikey looks away. Spits. "Okay
next time . . . You don't
get on my nerves before . . ."

Little Charlie waits,
with a look of imitative
indifference, says nothing more.

Pennies from Heaven:
Wham
Bam

A lush shadow-shape
answers Ikey's knock,
calls back in the house,
"Baby! your boy
back, again."

Ikey turns to me, rooted
in the unkept yard, winks.

Our daddy, holding the screendoor open,
leans easy on the off-
plumb frame, red braces heisting
his pinstriped, yellow slacks.

They speak, low, familiar, like man
to man; him watching me
with hand-shaded eyes. He signals.

"Hey," he says, and rubs
my head with his woman-soft hand.
"Taking care your mama good?"
"Yes, sir — I guess."
He nods a minute, looks away,
then: "Want a dime?" Hollers
back into the house,
"Eula! Bring me a dime here.
Go on in there, boy,
she'll give you one."
                    *

Inside as untended
as the yard. Blue raw
riffs drift from another room.

The woman, housecoat open, titties
lulling in her dusk-pink slip,
enters from where the victrola plays,
enters, humming, through the glass-
bead curtain — baubled strands rolling
and sliding about her mulatto body
like drops of jeweled sweat.

"So. You his other boy, huh?
And a Charles, too, named for him."
She laughs inside herself. "Hope
for your sake
that's all you got of his."

Then, without consideration or
shame, reaches down, in between her
ample, ample, yellow, yellowness,
rummages, then with her free hand
cups and hefts one,
a fresh-ripe fleshy fruit,
hefts, as if testing its
nubile weight.
(Rooted,
I could no more not look
than Mrs. Lot.)
Rummages, till, at last,
she fishes out a tatty
purse of coins.

"Close that damn screen," she calls,
making me remember they, too,
are in the world, "or this place'll

be full of flies." Says it
soft and easy, soft
and easy as lullabies.
It slams behind them as they
move, talking, out into the yard.

"He say a dime?"

Eyes groping; them nipples
big and poking,
I nod, dumb as Adam's ox.

Cool coin in my feverish palm.
Mouth
cotton-dry.
"Thank you—ma'am."
"Manners, huh? Here,
have another. Hell, they's
mine much as his. More,
for that matter.

But still, that second one's
our secret, . . . hear?"

Swear on the spot
not to never spend it. Never.
Not no time in my life.
*

"Don't tell your mama
where you got it,"
Papa warns me after, "or
where you been."

And, to Ikey, says,
"See you soon . . ."

'Round Midnight

circa late 20s

Black as Hell's chimney
soot, it glideswoops in
to roost, hunker-perched,
like a secret, claws
clenched 'round the footrail
of my bed. Then — its

grave respiration
controlling the twinge-
pulse in my maw — waits,
rapacious, ready
to ravish, to wrest.

I lie, cocooned in
petrification,
too terrified to
shriek or whine — until
the rooster rises,
crows. I sense the fear-

bringer blink. I roll,
with panic-strength, off
and under my bed,
to drowse swaddled in
bed clothes, knees to nose.   5

Fine and Dandy
circa 1933-35

Join up with us, says
Alonzo Lewis,
Master of Lincoln
High School marching band.

Says it because he
sees the need — and loans
the baritone. But

no son of Addie's
is about to be
tromping and stomping,
tooting while toting
no heavy horn wrapped
'round to weigh' him down.

The alto is light,
little and pretty,
so, one of those is
perfectly good enough.

Meandering
A Poem in 3 Movements

I. Merry-Go-Round
II. Dark Shadows (Take 1)
III. Hallelujah

" . . . Forth I wander, forth I wander,
And drink of life again."

"Fragment of a Greek Tragedy"
— A.E. Housman

I. Merry-Go-1Round

circa 1934

Kaycee night tripper
breaking my mama's rule;
underage I creep, unblinking
up blue-devil main drags
and down hootie-blue back alleys
that never sleep; listening
for answers, while I peep
through a haze of rot gut,
tea smoke and riffs,

at rough and ready
Shake Dancers,
Drag Acts,
and boogie woogie whores
raising sin.

The jazz and blues
jumping razorsharp,
or busting funky
from every portal and pore
of every jiving joint
and highballing sepian stomper,
hoping
to wrap their troubles in dreams,
or jump some sorrowful or saintly some
body or soul on
or off their minds.

I listen, learning
lessons of all kinds:
of eros, of charity, of choler,

and of cool, then
bustling back
before mother Addie returns
from nightshift charwomaning
to pack her eight o'clock scholar
off to school.

II. Dark Shadows (Take 1)

At an alley exit
listens; espies the clientele. One
in particular
for no particular reason. — Perhaps
the out of town cut of his clothes,
or the heed others pay (greed
sheening their skin
like dog days sweat). Knowing

they crave some-
thing of him,
he's disdainful as a school-yard bully
in a game.
Barrel bellied,
red veins vining his talcumed cheeks, he's
like a callous Santa Claus. — A buyer
perhaps, a banker
from back east? or
a big time politician
with a pocket full of strings.

As the music chants and moans
they puff, swill,
gorge on cigars, rye,
and two inch T-bones,
blood-rare.

Declaiming their delight,
they hunch each other, holler,
Ohh shimmy-shake! Come on mama,
shimmy-shake that thing for me!
and pat their feet

31

to some beat
that is nowhere in that room.

When done
slap the money down,
pat the waitress on the butt,
command: "Save a little
for the niggers in the band."

III. Hallelujah
circa 1934

There is evil going on on 12th Street.
>   *Tell it.*
>   A hornet's nest of iniquity,
>   *Well —*
Satan's play land,
>   lined with places where
red lights blaze both day and night.
>   *All right —*
>   They call them honky-
tonks. They call them dance
>   halls and and
cabarets and show bars and saloons.
>   *Well —*
>   But what they is is
is gin mills and brothels,
>   gambling dens and buckets-of-blood.
Hell halls,
>   *Un huh —*
>   where they play music
called boogie woogie and the blues,
>   *Well*
>   jazzed up till it burns like brimstone
>   *un huh —*
and is played by men
>   who ain't nothing but —
>   *Tell it.*
but the bringers of bad news.
>   *Yes.*
>   And that's cause Satan his-self
is the leader of them boogie woogie
>   bands.

Yes, sir.
All right.
Tell it.
And, because Satan will
    tempt the weak
       Un huh —
and the weary,
       Won't he?
and and will test the Stout
and the Strong,

      Say it
they parade down there,
    like lost lambs
      Yes —
like file shavings
     Un huh
drawn to a lodestone of lust;
      My Lord
men looking for strutting
    mincing footed women
     Un huh
    and women looking for boasting
    transgressing men.
      Yes
And neither of them don't care
    nothing about *howsomeever,*
or or or or about *wheresomeever,*
     Un huh
or neither *who-someever*
     All right
    Just as long as they can hear that
blue Devil music
     Yes
    and do the low down things
what it make them do

Don't you know
Don't you know
Don't you know.
And they don't *care*
Tell it —
They will take the baby's milk money
Well —
Will take anything
ain't on fire or nailed down
Uh huh
to get money to to to to
go down there
Yes
and and and drink it up,
Yes they do
or or or gamble it away,
Yes they do
shooting them craps;
Well
with dice carved from the bones of Christ
Well
Or or or they throw it away
on loose women
Well
scarlet women
Well
wanton, made up, low down
loose living, soliciting women
Tell it
or or or or they they they
waste it away on them reefers
or that cocaine, morphine or heroin
right down there on 12th Street

in the heart of Boss Pendergast's
　　　Sodom-like section of sin.
　　　　　Amen

But let me tell you
　　　All right —
　　　Let me warn you about something:
that cutting and shooting
　　　and carousing can't continue.
The Lord don't stand for
　　　but so much.
　　　　　Sure don't
And, oh my oh my when the dust do settle
　　　and, oh,
all the ashes is cool
　　　　Well
and the last notes of music
　　　have waft-ed on the wind
　　　　　Yes
those left standing
　　　will be none but
the children of the Lord.

They amened.

2.
If that's all that be left, young Charles
smirked,
won't be worth the stay
no way.

Hot House
1515 Oliver Street
      K.C., Mo.
           circa 1936-37

Circled, like cats on
eggs. Sparks crackled, hair
bristled when they brushed.
Addie. 33:
Mother. Rebecca
Ruffing Parker, 4
years his senior: Wife.
And baby Leon
Parker, whom Addie,
in course, of course, will
rear. But, what is that
to him? Charles Jr:
Baby-man. Groomchild.
Father. But 16.
But what is that to
him? Leave them, mother
and wife, under the
same roof, Addie's of
course, to decide how
many mothers are
enough; leave them to
find the harmony,
to follow his lead.

Carvin' the Bird
circa 1937

"Taking good care your
mama?" I nod yeah.

"Heard you the other
night; that joint, Dante's,
couple doors down from
the Jersey Hotel."

I'd seen him too. Him
and a brownskinned girl
calls herself Adelle.
"You might can play all
right," Charles Senior says,
"but you ain't got shit
to say; tweet-tweeting
little mockingbird,
too pitiful to
let loose the limb an'
take wing. You gotta
get from under your
mama, boy, find yo
own story to sing."

Licking hot sauce from
his fingers, says, "And,
oh, one more thing, then
you can go: you can
lend me five, till the
next time I come to
listen at you blow."

I Get a Kick Out of You

1. "The kick," they call
it, because it is.
A ball. Fist balled. Arm
in a necktie noose,
vein throbbing like a
good morning hard-on.

2. Thinks: ". . . *There's bound to*
be something else . . . hear
it sometimes. . . ." Twinkle-
tinkling shards of sound.
Kaleidoscopic
temptation that be-
sots from beyond the
metes and bourn of my
meager mastery.

Home Cookin':
Charles and Rebecca. Their Bedroom.
Evening.

circa '37

. . . says, "You won't come see
me play." "Could say the
same to you," she says.
"What? Where *you* be for
me to come?" "Right here.
Home. Where you belong."

He balls up his fist
and makes a face. "Why
you won't? I play good,
you know." "You spoiled and
want it all your way.
And I hate them joints,
I told you." Pauses.
"Addie hate them too."

He shoves her to the
wall. Advances. "You
leave my mama out
of this." "She in it,
like in ev'ry-thing."

He slaps her. "She in
it now?" "Yes." Slaps. "Now?"
"Still! — *And*, she know you
got girlfriends, know you
taking dope." His hand
hooks around her throat.
"How?" "Because I told

on you." Squeezing. "You
fixing to tattle
this?" "She know," she gags.

"Charles," Addie calls, "Charles,
you all right, up there?"

He backs away. "I'm
fine, Mama. We just
playing." A pause, then
she calls, "Mama's got
dinner ready. You
come and eat before
you go, now, you hear?"

Body and Soul
    (Take 2)

              "Abandon all hype
              ye who enter here."

        "A session for *the* cats,"
        Jo Jones, Basie band's
        Drummer Deluxe
              &z
        Main Man,
        thinks. "Congregation
      of the horn men of plenty
      in a year-'round town
    where musicians are apostles,
        jazz is gospel,
   and jamming's a communal rite.
          But,
      a breech of the bond
dictates a baptism on the killing floor."

        Circa spring '36.
    A Reno Club spook breakfast,   7
began about 5 a.m. The long room, more box car than
jazz joint; tables jammed so tight the wide hipped
waitresses threaten to upset them as they serve.
Musicians line the walls and bar, digging, sipping, or slip-
ping to sample the chippies' wares on tap
right upstairs; biding time till they can board the
bandstand and sit in for their ride on Jo Jones' bread
and butter 4/4 from his cymbal and snare.

Charlie, third year freshman, eases in, like an apology
slipped under the door. "Papa Jo presiding," he thinks.
"A killer-diller in high waist pants.
Plays piano. Sings and dances

like my daddy, asks no favors,
takes no shit, and don't apologize."

        Spies child Charlie as he sidles in.
               "Brat.
        Stray biddy in a brier patch,"
        Jo thinks. "Kid-man. Cocky
        and underfoot. But burning
            to be tolerated
        in our fast company . . ."

"To be able," Charlie thinks, "and
to do it with their ease. Their
joy! Till the measure
ain't can I run or bat, or conjugate
'a-mo, a-mas, a-mat'; ain't whether
I'm a mama's boy."

            "We
        call it playing," Jo thinks,
        "and it is, but it ain't,
        not just. We're Masters.
      We testify in disparity's face.
        We strike
        the common chord."

"Missionaries of cool," Charlie thinks,
"cuffs cutting the shoe tops
just so. Hats cocked, eyes squinted
against upcoiling smoke. Each
his own man
in his own way. Handles music,
liquor and sex
like they were his idea from way back."
*

"Laying down this fine-tuned rhythm," Jo
thinks, "regular as a 17 jeweled
Swiss movement railroad ticker,
tocking our open throttle rambling
and rocking to the land of Goshen
on the sweet swinging chariot
called the Daybreak Express."

"Prophets
of the mute parlance," Charlie thinks.
"Critique by stance, shrug,
or a motion of the mouth. A nod
is worth a week of words."

"And we testifying
and swinging!" Jo thinks.
"Letting our notes anoint
as we blow the blue demons
right on out the joint."

"My turn," Charlie thinks,
having finagled a chance.
Begins to blow.

"Who 'llowed this
ill armed Daniel
in our lion's den?" Jo thinks.
"Arsenal of nothing but nerve.
Don't know a key
from an apple core;
changes from a cow pie; his ass
from a coconut. Barely ready
to have his little say with the locals,
yet taking up a man's time;
hoping to short cut
into this line of elites. Who

44

raised this Negro! Ain't he got no daddy?
to tutor him to the commandments,
the stone etched etiquette
of our hierarchy of hip."

"I'm struggling, but I'm blowing,"
Charlie thinks. Impetuous.
"They got to admire that."

"Listening to no-
damn body but himself," Jo thinks.
"I'll warn him, enough
of nothing
is enough."

Impervious, Charlie thinks:
"Blow and show them
I will find the symmetry.
Strike the balance
within myself. Be a man
'mongst men. Just
like them."

"Tried to let him off easy," Jo thinks.
"Gonged with a couple of chiding cymbal shots;
sign even a disrespectful rookie
oughta recognize. But this
lesson-lacking misbegot's
forcing the affront,
flaunting his mannish ignorance
of manners he should've learned
with his mammy's milk. School's
OUT!"
*

The cats and customers
steel themselves
for the spanking
the fledgling's 'bout to get.
"Got it coming.
Hell, couldn't take a hint." But
where the code calls for indirection
Jo's anger and action shock . . .

As Charlie, horn still in his mouth,
steps back, bowing,
anticipating approval, applause . . .

Their fingers in their ears
they watch the hurled cymbal
slicing the air with its razor edged intent.

. . . he hears the cymbal clap,
KLACT-O-VEED-SED-STENE!

Feels his sphincter, dick,
and gut spasm, shrivel;
tastes lead-vomit-like metal
as the cymbal, Doom's Day's roulette wheel,
ringing, rimming round and round (will,
like unkept promises a parent made)
resound and resound;
will
randomly rip him
chilled and trembling
from reverie, gentle sleep
or sweat-soaked stupors.

They slap their thighs
and hold their sides. Weep.

*

Escaping, he sees his name
writ large in their book;
not inductee, but goat. Butt.
Altar meat.

Wrap
Your
Troubles
in Dreams

"The kick"
(the
musicians
word
for it):
benzedrine, marijuana, heroin, or
morphine. Good for him now and again,
he thought.
Dulled
the pulse
of a
sufferable
ache.
But think
what Addie
would say
if she
saw him.
"Charles?"
she'd say.
"What, mama?"
he'd answer.
"You best
leave
that stuff
alone."
"But Mama,
they
told me
it'd

make me
play
oh so
good."
"Please,
son, no.
You
sound
good to
mama
n
o
w
.
"

The Song Is You

"Music is feeling, then, not sound . . ."
  — Wallace Stevens, "Peter Quince at the Clavier"

Prof, who wasn't, but   8
conducted himself
that way, says, "I'm tired
of you draggin' 'round
like a scal'ed dog
in late December."

"He oughta knew I
didn't know better,"
Charlie pules. "Deserved
at least to be put
down the normal way."

"Got the blues? 'cause *you*
goofed not mindin' your
Ps an' Qs. Joe spanked
you with the hick'ry
you put in his hand."

"Still, didn't have to
do me like he done."

"World ain't your tit, boy.
This music's 'bout more
than wantin' to. 'S'bout
the feelin's of a
man pushed through his horn.
No cribbin', jivin',
nor connivin' like
you used to. It's like

with a goose, nothin'
but shit in you then
that's all can come out.
Otherwise any
child could do it. Grown
men wouldn't get the
privilege nor joy.
Now, get in step or
step on out the way."

Charlie thinks, Ain't my
daddy, can't tell me
what I ought to do.

Prof: "You want, I'll help."

"Okay," Charlie says,
plotting his revenge.

Repetition

>   (Take 1)

>   ". . . he went up into the
>   mountain . . ."

>   —Lester knows his horn, they said.   9
>   —Be holding a conversation, with plenty to say.
>   —Got 'im a sound fresh as next week's news, sweet
>   as a spinster's sachet.
>   —Solos unwind like a big ball of yarn.
>   —Like a schoolgirl in slippers chasing butterflies
>   in the amber beams of the moon.
>   —*Always* in control.
>   —*Knows* his horn!
>   —And *swings*.
>   —*Had better*! with Jo Jones behind him.
>   —Man, Lester ain't stud'in' Jo. Hell,
>   was a drummer *his-self*.
>   —*And* his daddy was a musician, traveled with carnivals
>   and minstrel shows.

>   Charlie thought:
>   "I'll be like the best, I'll be like Lester.
>   Then we'll see what the bastards have to say."

In pursuit, he insisted; not exile
nor contrition, took a summer band gig.
An Ozarks resort nestled on a lake.
The open air dance pavilion was decked
with colored bulbs and crepe-paper streamers.
*

Every non-working hour Charlie, like
a punished dunce, practiced (woodshedding, the
musician's word for it) playing along,
with Basie's new Vocalion platters;   10
his 70 cent tuition to the
University of Lester Young.
Lester soaring high above the band's blue,
loose and juicy riffs, while Charlie, repeating
the notes by rote, again and still again,

hoping some Lester rubbed off, some sunk in.

Things to Come

Basie and Lester's
discs repeating, re-
peating; as Charlie
nods; as after his
compelling Addie's
repeated telling
of lulling bedtime
tales; as becharmed as
by an endangered
damsel's entreating
from a realm beyond.

He is a-nod at
the arrival of
the Fresh Air cab with
visitors three, to
the Star-Lit Never
Land of Oob-Bla Dee.

"We," says the driver,
"are known by a list
of known as's long
as (as blues singers
sing) their right arm." We
be witches one place;
Trimurti; Wise Man;
or the Trinity
some place else," explains
the portly one, his
derby atilt, his
stogie unlit. Next,
in Dixie colonel's

hat and black string tie,
the third is heard: "For
now, think Mystic Knights
of the sea: Amos,
Andy, and Kingfish,
and that's who we'll be."

If not wisely but
too well, Charlie sniffs:
"Sirs, if peddling Pearls
of Wisdom praising
by-gone's values be
your plan? then I pray
thee, cast them before
swine and be gone. For,
Sirs, you see, I seek
to slay dragons; sing
Me: be Modern Man."

"We're here," Andy riffs,
"with prophecies, and
gifts. You'll be Three-Cheered.
Hailed Highest Hipster
of the New Jazz Hill.
Will get kicks, booty,
be revered." Charlie

smirks, "I'm deserving"
(without explaining
his rationale) "of
more than your forecasts
of wonders practice
will make me master
of in time." Kingfish
*

"Huumms," then narrows his
eyes, like a mongoose
measuring a side-
winder for size. "See,"

Charlie says, "I know
straight's crooked, crooked
straight. Believing else-
wise is asinine.
Life's lessons are just
prattled bed-tales crammed
with rage and clatter,
told so toddlers'll
toe the line." Kingfish
thinks: Best beware, boy. When
taken as rations,
gifts received with words
untender render
repasts distasteful
and mean, for they are
seasoned with rancor,
simmered in spleen. The

three caucus: Will the
gift they've brought come to
nought in the employ
of this misallied,
green, hobbledehoy?

"To be deserving
this jackdaw must learn
to cease disserving
himself," they decide.

Resolve: "Grant a taste
of what jazz and blues

ABCs is, then
defer his dreams till
the griper has paid
his piper for his
doing only as
he damn well pleases."

Out of Nowhere

1. Whispers: *"Listen:*
hear here, here, there; hear?
not just the line, the
notes; between, behind."
How the sounds take the
air, graceful as flushed
nightingales (or, as
Addie would claim, the
soul of Jesus, or
answerable prayers).

The power of guile-
less grace startles him:
perception in an
abracadabra
instant: answering
the mystery of
the mastery of
form, and content, and
approach. 2. Charlie
rouses, gropes for his
horn like an infant
for its nipple, mouths
the reed, blows. Practice
must make perfect, he
concludes, nodding, too
too pleased with himself.

Move

Charlie eye-balls the dentist's,
butler's or maybe
mortician's daughter, "Way
out of his league," as he noodles
through some 'sweet' band chart
soft and empty as the moon.

Snug in the embrace
of Negro *noblesse*,
she sedately shuffles
with a son of Kaycee Colored Society,
groomed to one day
commerce with wealthy whites.

Yet Charlie knows
beneath the Proper
she has an itching,
to leap clothed and giggling
into the lake, or
break into a common jitterbug; an itch
intense as his
to be admitted in Kaycee.

The next number,
a jumping blues, prompts
abstentions from the eldest and
Most Well-Bred, but
after quiet resistance
the Alpha Phi Alpha man indulges her.

My turn, Charlie thinks. Begins,
quoting "Ain't She Sweet?" pulling

a snigger from the boys, then
his heated choruses, coupling his hunger
with ingested lessons from Lester,
spark reflexive responses from her:
Socially no-noed shoulder hunches
and twists of hip, moves
as tabooed as loud or vaudeville;
but
are maiden testimony
to his move

from kid
to can.

This Is Always

— Tell me Prof put 'is foot in 'is butt.
— Sen' 'im off, tail 'tween 'is legs.
— Wa'n' gone but a minute.
— But go 'bout it now mo' like 'e mean it.
— 'N' puttin' 'is little notes together real nice.
— Still wild, now.
— This is always.
— Pay *no*body no min'.
— Irregardless.
— 'S that damned *habit*.
— Still . . .

Bird Feathers:
Why'd the Chicken Cross the Road?

CHARLIE
(screamed)
Piggy, stop!

PIGGY   11
(stopping on a dime
it seemed)

BUDDY   12
What? a cop?

CHARLIE
Put this hearse in reverse.
There's a chicken back there
I got to get, my man.

BUDDY
I see him. Laid out like a feather fan.

PIGGY
Too slow as he strode
'cross the road.

CHARLIE
Got to be fas', 'r
somebody bound
to run over your ass.

BUDDY
Reckon that yardbird walked when he should've run.
Played chicken with you, Piggy, just for fun.

*

PIGGY
Well the contest is over.
Look like I won.

BUDDY
Maybe Charlie feeling holy
thinks the bird's just doing po'ly.

PIGGY
Charlie think the bird ain't dead,
just stricken.

BUDDY
Naw, man, Charlie's hungry
wants to eat that chicken!

PIGGY
All this negro like to do is play music,
eat chicken and ball.

BUDDY
You going eat 'im now, Charlie,
feet, feathers and all?

PIGGY
Or take 'em on home
for your mama to fry?

BUDDY
Either way Charlie serious,
dig the look in his eye.

*

CHARLIE
Love me some yardbird that's no lie,
and can't blow a chance for a free taste,
let that fine fat fryer go to waste.

BUDDY
I hear you, man. You ain't said nothing but a word. Yard-
bird loving Charlie.

PIGGY
Yeah, Charlie Yardbird.   13

Body & Soul
>(Take 3)

A band of men: clan
of young Kaycee blues
blowers, who whooped, whored,
barreled along tarred
two-lanes town to town;
hellish fun loving
breed, wild as loco
weed; huddled around
the microphone, like
hobos about a
flame; fedoras and
top coats flung on chairs
and table tops with
ashtrays, Co'-Cola
bottles and coffee
cups. (Flasks lived on their

hip.) "My turn," Bird thinks,

and cocksure eases
into it, like from
a soft shoulder on-
to the interstate;
and when the rubber
meets the road, floors it,
kicking up a cloud,
which, in hindsight, will
remind them of a

prestidigitaled
puff of sorcerer's
smoke, or flourish of
his splendorous cape.

Dark Shadows

Take 2
(After an imagined
Edward Hopper painting)

1. Bird pats his foot
and hums the driver's
curses bullying
the infirmed band bus
across the flatlands;

hums the cross rhythms
of passed telephone
poles and near bald tires
rubbering road noon-
hot at 4 a.m.;

making time: the last
couple hundred home.

Bird pats his foot, hums
the feeble breeze's
weak relief, the sweat-
wet band's fitful snores,
intestinal grumbling,
and mumbled appeals
of, "But *Ba-by* , . . ." to
dreamed girl friends and wives;

pats his foot and hums
the axle and springs
rock-rattle over
rails and ties, then the
gnashing gears groaning

in downshift, the break-
shoes griping whine, the
cinder and gravel-
crunching settling sigh.

The sign: GAS GOOD EATS
WE'RE OPEN ALL NIGHT
The boys wake as one.
Feast and relief fox-
trotting in their heads,
but still they're alert
as a bus of black
men in the nineteen-
thirties Kansas night.

Bird pats his foot and
hums the fevered hush.

The cafe's face is
a mask of metal:

LUCKIES TASTE BETTER

DRINK COCA COLA
IN BOTTLES   ICE COLD
The pause that keeps you
going   BULL DURHAM

DO YOU BELIEVE IN
JESUS CHRIST? WE DO

A hand painted board:

STEAKS/SANDWICHES/HOT
ROAST BEEF/HAMBURGERS

*

And another sign
stating WHITES ONLY

Bird pats his foot, hums:
it begins at brains'
root, like an intro,
vamped, swelling with each
measured breath, the rests,
throbbing like pulse-pause
anticipations,
bode climax or death.

2. She comes outside.
The screen door eases
shut like an eye lid.
She stands, in ghost-thin
cotton, bathed in the
100 watt pool
cast from overhead.

Smokes, and fans with a
piece of white pasteboard.
Her eyes, inshadowed
by the light's angle,
are like road-tar chunks.
Hair, nails, lips, tip of
cigarette, scarlet
as the flying horse
and gasoline pumps
lined like red coated
guards with full-moon heads.

She is fleshy, yet
puts them in the mind
of a polished bone.

69

*

In her own time she
looks up, faces them
from her solitude.

In the sharp embrace
of her resigned gaze
they sweat, still as stones,
as if movement would
ignite the night, call
wrath down on the world.

Bird nods, pats his foot,
hums a funky blues.

Groovin' High

1. Legendary
horn men, light-trav'ling
to Boss Pendergast's
wide open, cattle
slaughtering outpost,
like gun-wise drovers
at drive's end; swagger
to showdowns at jazz
joints on bandstands size
of a postage stamp.

2. "Any new young
viers to face my
fire?" one asks. 3.

". . . my turn," Bird thinks. The

other, still sporting
his hat and coat, shows
in fact and effect
his lack of fear or
respect; postures for
a grinning gal with
big stockings and a
feather in her cloche.

Bird's senses, nimbled
by heroin and
the studied scoff, leap:
a giddy witted
whirl swirling into

the heart of their blues
blower's Battle Royal —

4. "Parker, huh?" the
other pants, once the
tune is through; coat 'cross
a chair, hat band black
with sweat. "Yeah, Yardbird

Parker. Who *were* you?"

Now's the Time
(Take 1)

(Bird's First Flight)

A Poem in 3 Movements

I. Celerity
II. Now's the Time
III. After You're Gone

"Now is the time
in spite of the 'wrong note'
I love you. My heart is
innocent."

"The Orchestra"
— William Carlos Williams

I.
Celerity
 (*circa* 1937)

1. Drizzly dawn. She

squats over a ditch
peeing at weedy
roadside's edge. Wears smoked

glasses, dark as dried
bloodstains; stark against
her sun-less white skin.

With motor running,
perchpoised young Bird waits,
arage to take wing,
to soar. 2. Later,

beneath dark stares, she'll
be, behind the shades,
a stone; listening; his
jazz jarring as Jack
Johnson's hook and jab.

II.
Now's the Time

1. Later. Mama
say, "You know what hour
it is, Charles?" And me,

doing my best to
just stand up straight, say,
"Mama, this a fan
of mine. And a friend."
I winked, I think. "Real
good friend." Mama nods,

arms folded, cutting
her eyes at the gal's
ways, corn-silky hair,
and thin little dress
could near 'bout see through.
"How do you do?" So
proper forget all
about her greasy
headrag and holey
housecoat. "I'm just fine,

Mama Parker." The

"Mama Parker" stop
her a minute. She
almost like that. And

then the gal say how
proud Mama must be,
account of how good

I can play, and say
how much she like it
and every-thing.

And me, my head is
going ninety miles
a minute, I say
we going in my
room a little while,
"Come on." Mama's eyes

squint like clenching fists.

Me, I'm 'bout through time
we get in there. 2.

"Common. Nothing but
trash," just like I knew
she'd say. And how it
didn't look nice, and
making my bed hard,
and what I want to
fool with her in the
first place for, and how
she'd even rather
I go be back with
Rebecca. I laughed.

"Charles, you can't learn to
leave their women and
that stuff alone then
it's time you got on
away from here. Now
listen to Mother:
no matter what, you
still a blackboy, and

them men will take you
with them, and you won't
come back. So, it's time
you go, 'fore they take
you away from me
for real." Head spinning,

eyelids heavy as
lead, "Yes Ma'am''s what I
think I must have said.

III.
After You're Gone

Later. Down to their
singlets, two 18th
and Vine jammers still   14
swinging, striving for
Strutter's Rights. Bird is

blowing his bye-byes,
his bound-for-brighter
lights blues. Her drink down

to warm water she's
tonguing her gold tooth
and wondering whose
hand'll halt them blue
devils hauling that
low burying ground
feeling t'ward her heart.

His train be done rolled
by daybreak; reckons
she'll sweep her welcome
mat, bathe, grease, powder;
leave her front door cracked.

Dark Shadows: (Take 3)
"Nighthawks"   15
      (circa '37)

1.
Jelly Roll Morton laid claim
to the creation of jazz, and
George Gershwin died of a brain tumor, Bix   16
Beiderbecke of the bottle, and Bessie Smith   17
of bias and bleeding on a Memphis back road;
Sweet music was slipping,
and Swing was starting to pay: 80

million on dance music in '37;
mainly the Lindy for the hep; like   18
up at the Savoy, when   19
Chick Webb's boys ambushed and   20
bashed Benny Goodman's men;   21
luckily the riot police
were on hand to contain the joy;

and the jitterbug and unauthorized jamming were   22
banned in Chicago, where
James Petrillo, local head
of the American Federation of Musicians was
the world's highest paid labor boss
at 500 bucks a week; Martha Ray   23
pulled 5 thousand per, but musicians
making 54 or more a week on one gig
couldn't moonlight, the union said.
54 dollars, that was. 2.

    In shadows black as
    blues, Bird, bedraggled,

skulked, avoiding the
harsh swash of light from
PHILLIES luncheonette,
where time killers bide
over coffee and
cigarette, and the
cunt-capped counterman
draws refills and swaps
cordial eatery
etiquette. Bird skulks,
waiting on a mooched
Manhattan bound band
bus ride, while back home —
where whims and wants were
nagged but indulged — is
500 hoboed
miles from Chi Town; cold
to a ragged assed
17 year old
with a borrowed horn
can ingratiate
his way into a
session, then blow each
and every away;
but bullshit walks in
the Windy City
too; dependencies
and per diem still
take the spirit of
all things: cash money,
Honey. "Bread is your

only friend," Bird thinks;
has visions of the
Apple: addictions
excused, "erratic"

embraced. The Apple:
where my fortune will
unfold; my talent
will open pocket-
books, doors, minds, eyes and
thighs, he's been told. Bird

waits, shuddering. He
blows on his hands, stamps
his feet, and hugs him-
self against the cold.

Autumn in New York

Manhattan's skyline,
a beastbird, its back
spike-scaled like mountains,
rises against a
diorama of
soot and diamonds, borne
on Hell's golden-red
fire. Hunched against the

unseasonable chill,
Charlie meanders
Gotham's mythic streets,
listens for rhythms
keyed to the tempos
and agendas of
the metropolis,
rushing around him
like Missouri white-
water around a
river rock; or like
careening roadsters
with tommy-gunning
Public Enemies
on the running boards;
or subways screaming
beneath the Great White
Way, like loosed bats from
Hades' maze. Listens

for syncopations
from flatfoots with brogues
and nightsticks chasing

apple-swiping wise
guys past brownstone stoops
of contract player
ingenues longing
for the love of all
American Joes
officed in Times Square
skyscrapers. Listens

for themes attuned to
the babble of tongues
celebrating the
boroughs passion for
anonymity
and public display;
for the harmony
with knickered newsboys'
EXTRA EXTRA EXTRA EX-
TRAS! heralding sports
finals, financial
calamities and
foreign disasters.

Listens for the chords
to accompany
lengthening shadows
of gargoyles, pigeons,
fire escapes, pawnshop's
triple spheres, bridges;
and the cadence of
flashing marquees and
caravaning cabs
honking over rain-
slicked avenues. And,
*

as if sucked into
its cyclone-like swirl —

Bird eye-views the self-
loving seductive
megalopolis from
the center of the
eye of God; sees it's
black and white simple;
knows he'll witness some
sin put his Kaycee
sightings to shame; yet,
as if the bones of
his forbears were
grist and grout for its
foundation and cracks,
he is home, good guys
will win and justice
will prevail in the
final reel: THE END

> "I shall die in my nest,
> and I shall multiply my days
> as the phoenix."
> Job 29:18

Something to Remember Me By

"Doctor Faustus . . . said,
I will have my request,
and yet I will not be damned."

. . . Well then, now, welcome
to the Big Apple;   24
lucky you found me
to be your guide (the
shadow man says. He
smiles to himself, there
being no one to
wink at or hunch.) Your
first night, huh? Well your
heart may be in K.
C. but your young black
ass in the Apple
now, with me; (his laugh
is iridescent
and city slick as
oil on a gutter
puddle) but I can
tell you know what you're
doing, (leaning close)
just ain't learned your way
around. Lucky you
found me to be your
guide. From now on (he
promises) you won't
even have to look,
I'll be every-where.

(He steps back, surveys
me.) Welcome to the

*

Apple! (he repeats)
Zoo York's what I call
it: menagerie
of snakes and storks, bears
and bulls, Christians, apes,
dragons, and royalty
of every kind. Yours
truly always got
sweet music (he grins).
Guaranteed. For a
price I will provide
exactly what you
need. But you go'n do
all right, one day, can
look at you and tell.
Hell, here, a little
something to help you
on the way. Welcome
to the apple. Hope
you have a long and
a prosperous stay.

Scrapple from the Apple
Harlem, *circa* 1938

"Incline your ear, and come unto me:
hear, and your soul shall live; and I will
make an everlasting covenant with you . . ."
Isaiah 55:3

1.
"Ladies and Gentleman,
Harlem's
Jimmy's Chicken Shack
is pleased to present
the Master of Harmonic Chops,
the King
of cooking Rhythm,
the Chef de Cuisine of Swing!

Art
Tatum!"   25

God

is in the house
feeding His disciples
(the commons and the downtown swells)
a feast of full fisted cadenzas
and arpeggiated runs
arabesquing
through the kitchen smells and clatter,

where Bird,
in the scullery,
wipes his hands on his apron,

splotched from scouring
burnt and greasy pots and pans.

Bird thinks:
Back home
(12 hundred 8 miles southwest)
we catered to in-migrant musicians,
wouldn't let 'em spend a dime.

But months here
and I'm still scrappling,
greeted with Big
Apple in-
difference
and not playing one paying union gig
in all this time.

So, can't be no return to Kaycee Blues
with empty, wrinkled, pimp-soft hands, gray
from Dutch Girl Cleanser
and dishwater dues.

2.
Listening:
Tatum
ladling solo helpings
from his joyous stew of styles,
rechristening
every tune he touches
while
Bird, unbidden observer of the banquet,
smiles,
thinks:
Like listening
to begged lessons,
and bootlegged

89

Lester with Basie sessions
those weeks of Ozarks woodshedding
my first time out of Kaycee;
learning scales and chords by rote
with poetic Pres pulling my coat,
till I'd ingested his harmonic offerings
note
for note,

then returned
new-strengthened;
battered the breach of swingmatism's
elder battalions,
and garnered my first respect
with what I'd learned.

So, ain't no way to
go back, not now no how,
not tattered, hornless, licked,
cacooned in "couldn't do";
not the formerly hazed
mama's boy,
with no tales of sand raised
nor all-star asses kicked
at Minton's or the Savoy.   26

3.
Bird,
blue
and hungry for reassurance,
behind his hapless
Harlem scrapplings
and the humiliations Kaycee'd put him through,
listens,
gulping, heapings of the harmonic hosannas,
like a soulstarved gastronome.

But,
Tatum's funky figurations,
too raw-complex, too intense
to simply bear witness
to jive junkie justifications,
and mama's boy laments,

slice scythe-like
through the haze
of Bird's allegro-fortissimo-like
high, the maze
of his adagio-pianissimo-like
low, and spread,

till suddenly
as a bolt whistling at soundspeed
across the Kansas flatlands,
Tatum's sounds are a jolt,
a burning sign
like heroin's first sweet orgasmic spasm
down the lightning rod of Bird's spine;

affirming:
music of this magnitude,
the meat and bread of it,
where the idea of
love
is at least alleged,
and joy and surprise exude

is

at best
double edged,
*

it nourished,
he realizes (as with the comedown
from his first high),
but it consumed,

and therefore, is not,
as he'd presumed,
a shield against an appetite
prodigal and rapacious as his,
so is,
therefore
not salvation
not wholly blessed and bright,
nor will, till
endtime,
be fully famine
or feast,
but a perpetually panicked fare
of the creation and revelation
of his best

and least.

4.
Like God's ornamental embellishments
the realization sops into my broiling
bones,
spreads like prairie blaze
along the main streams of my blood.

and,
as if my fists were afire,
I thrust them
through the sink's steaming surface
afloat with grease, ortgrissle,
and bubbles shinybright as new-minted money.

Submerged
they burn like dry ice,
as if at the possibility of
my own
divinity
or damnation;

and thus baptized in that befouled font
my fingers unlock,

flex, as wings inhaling for lift,
and fiercely take the air,
dripping and dancing over the phantom keys
of my hocked horn
like wringing wet revival rejoicers
ecstatic at a fiery message from on high.

Silent,
optionless,
I "play"
led by this exalted blindman,
God,
complete within himself,
in harmony, in that moment,
with his clarity, brilliance and dexterity.

5.
But
now knowing,
even after hatching that haunting concoction
of Kaycee blueshuffle
and careening Big Apple speed —
dark
will still follow day,
Fall follow Pride;

nothing that
was
will be annihilated;
yardbirds
will still be fried.

6.
God is in the house,
and Bird, anxious for a smoke
busts suds
and listens to God's word
through the crashing cymbal-
like clatter and clamor,
full of sound, fury and signifying;

learns: From the father
proceeds the son.

Laughs.

Takin' Off

Residing at the Woodside: 27
   fiend foundling
    in the hurtling twirl
panic dancing temptation's razoredge.
Pops', Pres' and Tatum's lessons learned,   28
   but sick of the same old
   broken record changes
time and time and time and time again.
   Knows there's "bound
   to be something else . . .
   could hear it sometimes
   but couldn't play it . . ."

   Till
jamming that night with Buddy Fleet   29
   in that Chili joint
   when it hit me:
   WHAM.
Like a bowl full of benzedrine.
   BAM.
A new way how to swing
   from one note to the next:
   substitutions and resolutions
   begetting new themes
   inside and in-between
   them old time,
   old time-y
   Kaycee variations.

"The Bird of Time has but a little way
To flutter — and the Bird is on the Wing."
   —*The Rubaiyat of Omar Khayyam*

Back Home Blues

circa 1938

> "Some Are Born To Sweet
> Delight, Some Are Born To
> Endless Night."
> —William Blake

1. Not sure at first
(arriving during
the Acknowledgments,
trainsmoke in my clothes)
late, to witness this,
his final leaving.
Is it even him?
as wax-sallow as
false fruit, him, father,
man whose name I bear?

GOOD LUCK OLD BUDDY

trumpets the floraled
sentiments of his
sporting cronies. I
join Mama amidst
his admixture of
bedizened women,
strewn on the pews, gilt
blossoms plucked from a
poly-complexioned
bouquet. — God bless his

Two-timing soul, they
weep and holler, sling
tears and wring their hands.

God bless his tan and
dapper two-timing,
three-timing, four-five-
six, seven-timing
soul, God bless him! 2.

"Look at him," Addie
whispers, a warning.
"Look at him good. Who
let one cut him down,

God bless him; let some —
some strumpet cut him
down, just like a dog."

3. Just like a dog,
god damn you, now you'll
never know whether
I'm worth more than a
nod, a nickel, a
pat atop my head.

And I'll never have
the inheritance
of your approval;
familiar, man to
man. Only a drunk's
rambling endowment,
limp legacy: "Do,"
slurred one revelous
night. "Live. For now. 'Cause
life flashes past fast
as headlights 'round a
snake-curved mid-night road.
The Whoosh! 16th note

quick; the departing
taillights Satan's eyes,
promising: 'Dig you
now, catch you later.'"

Hootie Blues
  circa 1939

                    1.
              The musicians:
dark doublebreasteds creased and cleaned,
         black butterfly clip-ons
              alight on white
           heavy-starched collars;
          shoes, hair and horns
                 sheened.

              The crowd:
             race royalty:
Pullman porters, hustlers, butlers,
           and chauffeurs,
    rendezvous with their court:
barbers, shoeshiners and gofers:

                 and their
Vaselined, Nadinolaed and hot combed ladies: 30
       cooks, beauticians, mammies
               and maids
          powdered in shades
         of white, flesh, pink,
         brunette, and high-brown;
faux French *parfum* bouqueted;
       primped, plumed, arrayed
in finest finery and fake fox flings,

                indignant
   at having their night of freedom
          and fun delayed.
                    *

"Bird go'n' show?"
Buddy Anderson, the tenor, whispered.

"Wouldn't bet the rent money on it,"
trumpeter Orville "Piggy" Minor said.
"You a musician, Negro," Buddy countered,
"how you got rent money?"
"Didn't lend Bird nothing
this month," Piggy said, deadpan.
"One! two! . . ." Jay McShann, the leader
called Hootie,
counted off.

After the first set
Hootie fired Bird
again —
in absentia.
Again.
"I fucking give up!"

2.
Before the last set
Bird showed up, rucked
but recovering, penitent
as a shitty nosed pup.

Gene Ramey,
Dutch uncle, way paver, bassist,
gave Bird a look:
You too good
be doing the way you do.
Boy, that damn dope is ruining you.

"Bird," Hootie said,
"the tail
is wagging the dog. Now

you been my right hand:
arranger, soloist,
reed rehearser,
but I'm 'bout a hornplayer
like I'm 'bout a woman,
don't need one can't make time. Oh,
I'd love to listen at you every night,
but when I give the downbeat
is when you got to be here
to blow. So
till you can straighten up
and fly right,
what I got to do
is I got to furlough you."

Grinning his cherub grin
Bird agreed,
then blew two choruses of *Hootie Blues*
that made the whores homesick
and caused the Christians to wag their heads.

"See you in a week,"
Bird promised with a wink.

"Bet my rent against it,"
Piggy told Orville.

Orville laughed, "That's
what you think."

They Didn't Believe Me

1. Hootie's band blows.

Bird, horn in his mouth,
cheeks puffed out, nods. 2.

Glideswoops. Perched on the
music stand. They stare
into each other,
till the raptor blinks.

"How now?" Bird greets it.

"Don't you fear me still?"
it asks. "No." "Oh. So

how y'doing then?"

"I'm 19, I'm armed,
dangerous, getting
faster every day.
I'm never going
to die, and they like
me." "But you're spoiled, a

mama's boy, a mooch;
hand in *every*-one's
pocket (payback rare
as plumage on pigs).
You're self centered as
the sun; don't show up
for gigs . . ." "But, I blow
*

102

and they forgive my —
trespasses." Quotes the

raptor, "Hate the sin,
but love the sinner."

Dizzy Atmosphere:
Bird and Dizzy Meet
in the Booker T. Hotel
in Kansas City. 1939   31

1. Dope in Bird's tie
tied vein like salmon
in a spring stream. 2.

"Session for the cats
at the Booker T.,"
Buddy Anderson
said. "Some of Cab's band'll   32
be by, wanna go
'n' blow?" Bird deadpanned,
"Hidee- Ho." 3. "Diz,"   33

I said, breakfast bound
through the overstuffed
lobby, lit by shaft's
of morning sun, "you
play like me." "Likewise!"
"Maybe we can do
it again next time
you're in Kaycee." "Or
you're in the Apple,"
Dizzy said. "May-be."
Dizzy's words: ". . . in the

Apple . . ." scream now like
Manhattan taxi
horns through sewer steam.
*

4.   "— Ma'am?" Thought he heard
his mama calling
like a cymbal crash:
"Charles!" "Mama?" "When you
coming see about
your son?" "Aw, Mama,
you know he'll get the
better raising 'neath
your hand —" "When, Charles?" "Soon,
Mama," he promised,
nodding and grinning
his cherub grin, which
seemed to take a week.

Just Friends

Came once, Addie told me,
Charles Senior did, once,
while I "was gone."

One Sunday, before church it was,
and sober as a judge, she submitted
in his defense. Asked
about The Boy. Not
Ikey or me, but Leon,
the baby. His grandson.
My heir.

Played with him on the splintered porch,
while inside she did her primp and preen,
peeping past the curtains
and out the front door's screen.

Same porch
where I, her good boy, alone,
imprisoned, peered at the passing boys
as they jumped and joked their joys,
and my forlornness lumped and choked
like a half-swallowed knucklebone.
*

Charles Senior'd held little Leon's hands up high,
Addie told me,
and they'd laughed as he sang and danced
his old vaudeville mess — Like
back when we first met, she said —
Her little man
standing on his grandpa's feet;
they rollicked
like colts or kids in clover
and, made a joyful noise.

No different than me with Hootie's boys
the time we got high
off nutmeg and Pepsi-Cola . . .
In Wichita it was,
was just before the set
when they let me fix them up.
(Didn't take much convincing
them being as curious
as I was willing.)

And so, when Hootie gave the downbeat
didn't
no-body move!
 "And deep-asleep he seemed, yet all awake.
And music in his ears his beating heart did make."

Hootie cut his eyes
and cussed us through his teeth.

In our *"mild-minded melancholy"*
we, like a class picture, were solemn
and seated straight. Hootie
counted off again,
fighting flop-sweat and disbelief.

"*Let us alone,*" we grinned.
"*Time driveth onward fast,*
And in a little while our lips were dumb.
Let us alone."

"All right, goddamnit!"
Hootie blustered. "Now
what the hell?"
                          That
did it.
Our tottering tickle boxes
toppled,
we giggled like school girls
till we were weeping weak.

Hootie knew whatever'd been done
I'd had a hand, and damning my buffoonery
decreed I was banished from his band.

Months later, Piggy, snickering,
recalled Hootie's double-
take as we'd sat
still as whole notes, or
deacons during a wake,
releasing a fresh outbreak
of crows and cackles from the boys.

Best prank I'd *ever* pulled,
they tooted,
then, unanimous as Musketeers,
declared me All Star Jokester, *and*
Hornsman Most High!
*

and better than just *accepted*,
I was the apple
of their eye.

> "*To muse and brood and live again in memory*
> *With those old faces of our infancy* . . . ."

The Jumpin' Blues

Squares out there dancing
don't suspect a thing.

Got no idea
how strong a man got
to be t' drag (night
after night) up on
this bandstand, lift his
horn, push his raging
breath past this reed, through
this curving metal
cone; so I can blow
these jumpin' blues, and
they can rub and twirl.

I Want Ev'ry Bit of It

When Moses (brooder,
murderer, loner)
heard the call he did
not want to hear it.

Probably'd read ahead;
Job's chapter; his turn
to suffer God's whim.

Moses got a glimpse
of all the burdens
Job shouldered: stormy
weather; ridicule
from his back-biting
buddies; slaughter of
offspring and livestock —
and Job was perfect.

Who needs it? Moses
must've thought. Yeah, sure,
the recognition'll
be cool: kicks, toast of
my people, never
meet a stranger, host
of adulation
from womankind, peers.

— But being followed
everywhere; bushes
bursting into flames,
incendiary
demands . . . — But, still, Bird

*

thinks, chance to be all
things to all people:
prophet, free spirit,
style setter . . . Who, Bird

wonders, no matter
what the cost, who, in
their right mind, could
ever turn that down?

Now's the Time: (Take 2)
Bird, Apple Bound,
Boards the Kaycee Special
                    circa 1941

. . . perch-poised

like the menaced Poet at Hellsmouth,
beasts crouched at his back;

takes chilling measure
of the eversloping landscape,
mucked, moiled, writhing.

Optionless, but
drawn,

descends wholly

into the whirl . . .
                    " . . . Hold on
tight. Hold
tight, my honey. Ride 'em,
and hold on tight . . ."

Easy to Love

And he went up into the mountain . . .
And and and and and
he *de*-scended from from from
the mountain top
and and and and and the multitudes
I say the *multi-tudes*
they fell in behind. He came
down from being *up* up in
the mountain! And and and he came
down and they who had been
at the foot, *un-able* to
go up there, they were *waiting*,
wait-ing for his return.
They hadn't been *able*
to climb up, they had
too many
burdens to make the trip.
They were *bowed down*, so they *couldn'*
go up. They were bowed down with some
old different kinds of *de-fects*
and *de-ficiencies*. So when he
came down and and and and and
was *a-mong* them — That did it!
They changed his name! They they they
they changed his *name*, because because
he was new. He got new up on that
mountain top. He aspired. He
fit the battle. He he he
rose to to to to
a higher plane. When he went *up*
he was one somebody. But when he
came *down*, I say when he came *down*,

he was some-body *new*. And he brought
something new
with him. Yes he did. He
had went up
and he had been *disciplined*
and he had got in *harmony*. *So,*
he had to be new bap-*tized*, you see.
He was baptized in their belief. He he he
was was was baptized in their wonderment.
He was *baptized* in the name of the Father
and the son. You see.
And the disciples
were waiting
at the foot of the mountain
where the land was flat.
They gathered '*round*. They
circled him.
And he *taught* them. He *taught* them
what he had learned
at the top of the mountain,
what he had *learned*
at the *bottom* of the mountain,
what he had learned in between.
He taught them the *secret* things.
And as sheep having no shepherd
lost and astray the multitudes
the multi*tudes*
followed him.
And they followed him
and they *imitated* him.
And he was *pride*ful
and they followed him
and he was *vain*
and they followed him
and he was *de-mand-ing*
and they followed him

and he was *self-ish*
and they followed him
and he was *lust-ful*
and they followed him
and he was *glut-ton-ous*
and they followed him
and he was *vo-ra-ci-ous*
and they followed him
and and and and and
and they tried to be one
with him
be-cause
be-*cause*
be-*cause*
he *knew*,
and because he *was* new.
And he was new baptized.

Author's Notes:

I want to present the sense of what I, as an African American male writer, sense of the character of this man, Charlie Parker, African American male musician, filtered through the oral evidence of those who knew him according to whatever their standards were in regard to those things. What's here are, at best, impressions, through a veil of more than half a century, and not necessarily facts. Therefore, none of it should be taken as the *truth*. Okay? Cool.

1. Kaw: River which separates Kansas City, Kansas from Kansas City, Missouri.
2. "Oh, Oh, My, My": Tune recorded by Charlie Parker.
3. Chan Richardson: Parker's common law wife.
4. John "Ikey" Parker: Charlie Parker's half-brother.
5. "When I was a kid what I can remember best is rolling off the bed at night, pulling the covers down over me, bundling into them and rolling right under the bed for the rest of the night." ("Charlie Parker," *Jazz 1956*, p. 38.)
6. Thomas J. Pendergast: "Boss" of Kansas City, 1926-1939.
7. Spook breakfast: Jam sessions that began when after-hours joints closed. Food was available to early rising working people.
8. Prof: "Professor" Buster Smith, saxophonist, Parker mentor.
9. Lester Young: Influential tenor saxophonist, who played with Count Basie and his orchestra early in their careers. Nicknamed "Pres."
10. Vocalion platters: "Shoe Shine Boy," "Evenin'," "Boogie-Woogie," and "Oh Lady Be Good," recorded on the Vocalion label October 8, 1936. (Count Basie, piano; Carl Smith, trumpet; Lester Young, tenor; Walter Page, bass; Jo Jones, drums.) They sold for 35 cents apiece.
11. Orville "Piggy" Minor: Musician in one of Parker's early bands
12. Buddy Anderson: Trumpet player with the Jay McShann band.
13. "Yardbird": Charlie Parker's nickname, later shortened to "Bird."
14. 18th and Vine: Streets in the heart of the night club district of Kansas City.
15. "Nighthawks": A painting by Edward Hopper.
16. George Gershwin: American composer; Bix Beiderbeck: A white trumpet player with swing orchestras.
17. Bessie Smith: Black blues singer.

18. Lindy Hop: Popular dance during the era.
19. Savoy Ballroom: Popular Harlem night club.
20. Chick Webb: Black orchestra leader.
21. Benny Goodman: White orchestra leader.
22. Jitterbug: Popular dance.
23. Martha Ray: Pop singer and comedic actress.
24. "The Big Apple" (or "the Apple"): Nickname for New York City as a place of temptations.
25. Art Tatum: A famous virtuoso piano player, nicknamed "God."
26. Minton's/the Savoy: Harlem night spots which featured experimental BeBop music.
27. The Woodside Hotel: Parker's residence during his first stay in New York.
28. "Pops": Louis Armstrong's nickname.
29. Buddy Fleet: Guitarist.
30. "Nadinolaed": A reference to Nadinola, advertised as a skin lightening cream.
31. Dizzy: Dizzy Gillespie, an innovator of Bebop.
32. Cab's cats: Singer and band leader Cab Calloway and the men in his band.
33. "Hidee-Ho": Expression popularized by Cab Calloway in one of his songs.

About the Author

Bill Harris is well known as a playwright. Among his best known works are *Stories About the Old Days* , starring Abbey Lincoln in its original production, *Every Goodbye Ain't Gone,* starring Denzel Washington, and Robert Johnson: *Trick the Devil* and *Riffs*. His plays appear in such collections as *The National Black Drama Anthology*, *New Plays for the Black Theatre*, and *African American Literature*, edited by Al Young.

Currently an associate professor of English at Wayne State University, he was formerly production coordinator of Jazzmobile and the New Federal Theatre in New York, as well as chief curator of the Museum of African American History in Detroit.

Yardbird: Side One, combines Harris's love for jazz and theater.